Tantalizing Tamales

Rio Nuevo Publishers®
P.O. Box 5250, Tucson, Arizona 85703-0250
(520) 623-9558, www.rionuevo.com

Text and photography © 2007 by Rio Nuevo Publishers. Food styling
by Tracy Vega.

Photography credits as follows:
Mary Humphreys: page 80.
W. Ross Humphreys: front and back covers, pages 3, 5, 20, 32, 35, 44,
56, 68, 71, 79, 84.
Robin Stancliff: pages 4, 25, 31, 43, 49, 61, 64, 67.

Library of Congress Cataloging-in-Publication Data

Doland, Gwyneth.
Tantalizing tamales / Gwyneth Doland.
    p. cm. — (Cook west series)
Includes index.
ISBN 978-1-933855-03-5
1. Stuffed foods (Cookery) 2. Cookery, Mexican. 3. Cookery (Corn) I.
Title.
TX836.D65 2007
641.8—dc22

                        2007007553t/k

Design: Karen Schober, Seattle, Washington.

Printed in Korea.

10 9 8 7 6 5 4 3 2 1

tantalizing
tamales

GWYNETH DOLAND

COOK WEST
SERIES

RIO NUEVO PUBLISHERS
TUCSON, ARIZONA

introduction

Today, more than five hundred years after European explorers first reached the New World, it is almost impossible to imagine that until the sixteenth century, the Swiss had no chocolate or vanilla in their pantries, the Italians had no tomatoes, the Irish no potatoes, the Thai no chile peppers—and none had corn. All of these ingredients are native to the Americas, and though new to European explorers, they had been staples of the Mesoamerican kitchen for thousands of years. Corn, which now grows in nearly every country in the world, had been domesticated in the Americas some 5,000 years before Columbus's first visit.

Although we don't know for sure the exact origin of tamales, we can see from pots and carvings that for the ancient Mayans, tamales were their daily bread. (The word comes from the Nahuatl *tamalii,* and "tamal" is the correct singular form, although "tamale" is more common.) Researchers believe it is likely that tamales originated in Mesoamerica and eventually spread throughout the Americas and beyond. An ancient precursor to fast food, the supremely portable tamale provided a satisfying and nutritious meal for people on the go—and it still does. Tamales are a popular menu item in Latin American restaurants and market stalls, although for most home cooks, the time and effort required to prepare tamales (as opposed to tacos or burritos) means they are mostly made on celebration days. Christmas, New Year's Day, the Day of the Dead, weddings, birthdays, and baptisms are often celebrated with a feast of tamales.

In its most simple form, the tamale is made from ground corn that has been slaked with lime or lye and mixed with fat to make a sticky dough called *masa*. Portions of the dough are wrapped in corn husks or leaves and baked or steamed; although tamales are often served wrapped, the husks or leaves are rarely edible. Tamales can be eaten plain or served with salsa, chile sauce, or the unique Mexican sauce called *mole* (MOE-lay). Sometimes the dough is filled with bits of cheese, chicken, fried pork skins—or more exotic local ingredients like iguana. Dessert tamales can be sweetened with honey or sugar and flavored with things like raisins, cinnamon, and coconut.

For every country, every village, and every family that makes tamales, there is a different tradition, but for creative cooks, the mild flavor of tamale dough presents an empty canvas, inviting inspiration and experimentation. Expensive restaurants may fill their tamales with foie gras and garnish them with truffles, while a child making tamales with Grandma slips some chocolate chips into his dough. The possibilities are nearly endless. In this book you'll find some traditional recipes as well as some innovations, and after your first batch or two, you should feel confident enough to experiment with your own masas and fillings.

TECHNIQUE   *The Game Plan.* The process of making tamales is fairly labor intensive, and most cooks enlist at least a couple of family members or friends to help, forming an assembly line for production. If you plan on making more than a small batch— and really, it's not much more effort to make five dozen than it is to make one dozen—do yourself a favor and get help.

If you happen to live near a *tortillería* (where they grind corn for fresh tortillas and tamales), you may be able to buy *masa para tamales* there—just ask. Otherwise, you'll need to make your own dough from *masa harina,* or ground corn flour. Because the masa needs to rest for a while before it is ready to use, make it first (see "Making Masa" recipes, pages 20–30), then wrap the dough in plastic wrap and let it sit out for an hour or so. If something interferes with your cooking plans, you can refrigerate the dough for a day or freeze it for up to a month.

Most of these recipes make enough dough for two dozen medium tamales—mostly because it's harder to whip smaller amounts of lard, but also because making this amount isn't much harder than making one dozen. Most of the tamale recipes call for a half-batch of dough, assuming that you will either make two kinds of tamales or freeze any leftover dough for later. Both the dough and the wrapped tamales freeze well.

While the dough is resting, prepare the wrappers. Dried corn husks are the most common tamale wrappers, but they need to be softened before they can be used. You will notice that I suggest having more wrappers than you expect to need for each recipe, in case of breakage, which is fairly common. I like to put the husks in a tall, sturdy pitcher (at least 2 quarts) and pour hot water over them. After 15 or 20 minutes they're ready to use. Frozen banana leaves must be defrosted first, but either way—fresh or frozen and thawed—the leaves will need to be softened by holding them briefly over a flame. Banana leaves don't need to be soaked before using, and they impart a distinctive aroma and flavor to the tamales.

It is sometimes difficult to estimate exactly how much of the inside filling you'll need for a batch of tamales, but as a general rule it will be less than you expect. Only a tablespoon or two at most will fit inside the masa, so as a rough estimate, you can plan on making about a cup of filling per dozen tamales.

If you want to serve your tamales with homemade chile sauce or mole, I recommend you not attempt to make both in the same day—unless your kitchen is big and fully staffed with volunteers. A fresh salsa, however, won't take much time; you can whip one up while the tamales steam.

Composing the Tamales. When you're ready to put the tamales together, clear off the biggest table in the house and cover it with newspaper or a plastic tablecloth—this is going to be a messy job. At one end of the table, put the pitcher of soaking corn husks or a bowl of softened banana leaves. Next, place a bowl of the masa, then a bowl of the filling, and next to that a pile of corn husks or banana leaves, and extra strips for tying. At the end of the table should be a big cookie sheet or pan to hold the finished tamales. (If you're making a small batch by yourself, you can make do with a long stretch of counter space or a smaller table.)

The first step of tamale assembly is spreading the masa onto the wrapper. First, pull a corn husk from the soaking water and use your fingers to "squeegee" most of the water from it, then lay it flat on the preparation surface. If you don't mind getting messy, you can use your hand to spread the masa, but I find it's easier to use a wide spatula or a half-moon-shaped plastic dough scraper. Whatever tool you use, the goal is to spread three or four tablespoons of masa onto the wrapper in a tall rectangle about half an inch thick, being careful to leave at least one inch of masa-free border on all sides. The size of your rectangle will depend on the size of your husk, but aim for something at least 2½ by 4 inches.

If you've formed an assembly line, the designated "masa spreader" will now pass the smeared husk to the "filler" (filling is easy, so you can safely assign this job to an inexperienced member of the team). The only firm rule about filling is *never overfill a tamale.* Using a small spoon, the filler will spread a tablespoon or two of pork in red chile (or sautéed mushrooms or whatever you're using) in a line down the center of the masa. Now pass it on to the next station for wrapping.

To wrap the tamale, lift the long sides of the husk together towards the middle, so some of the masa falls over the inner filling. Drop the sides of the husk back down. Fold the bottom of the husk up over the filling and the top of the husk down. Rotate the tamale and fold the sides in over the center. Now take a long strip from one of the softened husks and use it to tie a "belt" around the middle of the folded tamale. There are many ways to wrap tamales, some simple and some fanciful. You don't always need to tie them, either. Sometimes you can just fold them over, depending on the size of your husks, and that will suffice. Feel free to get creative with your methods, just as long as you leave no more than one open end—you don't want the filling to leak out!

To cook the tamales you can use a steamer pot specifically made for the job (called a *tamalera*), a large canning pot, a lobster steamer, or any large-capacity pot with a steamer rack in the bottom. (If you don't have a steamer rack, wad up enough tangerine-sized balls of aluminum foil to cover the bottom of your pot; they'll elevate the tamales enough.) Pour water into the bottom of the pan, stopping half an inch short of the steamer rack. Gently add the tamales to the pot and bring the water to a boil, then reduce the heat and simmer, covered, for about an hour. Some people like to leave one end of the tamale open, in which case they need to stand the tamales in the pot with the open ends up; otherwise, you can just pile them on top of each other. Check the pot every 20 minutes and add more boiling water if necessary to keep it from running dry. (If you put a couple of pennies in the bottom of the pot, they will rattle as long as there's water simmering in there; when they stop rattling you'll know the water has evaporated.) You'll know the tamales are done when the dough peels away from the husk cleanly; if it sticks, cook them 5 minutes longer and check again.

Tamales freeze very well, so if you don't have time to steam all of them right away, you can store them in the freezer, tightly wrapped, for a month.

INGREDIENTS   *Masa* is the dough used to make tamales. Traditionally, it is made from lard, broth, salt, and dried corn that has been soaked with lime or lye, then hulled (you may know this as hominy, and in the Southwest it is sometimes sold as *nixtamal*). The slaked corn is ground while still moist, and the best tamales are made from freshly ground masa. Unfortunately, unless you live near a tortillería that will sell you "masa para tamales" (just ask nicely!), you'll have to make your own with masa harina, or dried masa flour. Look for masa harina (literally, "dough flour") in the Mexican or ethnic foods section of your supermarket, or at online retailers that specialize in Latin American foods (see Sources, page 86). You may also come across refrigerated masa in some stores; try it if you want, although I haven't found a brand I like as well as homemade.

Although ground slaked corn is most common, there are other interesting ways to form a dough for tamales. Green corn tamales, for example, are made with fresh corn and grits instead of masa. You can make a fine—if non-traditional— tamale from grits, which are just coarsely ground hominy. You can also use the kind of coarse-ground cornmeal that you might use to make polenta. Some tamales are made with potatoes or, more rarely, rice.

Lard has been the traditional fat used to make tamales since the Spaniards brought domesticated pigs to the New World.

Over the past century, some cooks switched to partially hydrogenated vegetable oil for health reasons, but now that we know about the dangers of trans fats, lard is once again the ingredient of choice. Unfortunately, the lard found in most grocery stores is hydrogenated to make it shelf stable; it also tastes terribly bland. If you can find locally made lard at your farmers market or specialty foods store, buy it. For a real treat, make your own lard: Ask your butcher for several pounds of fresh pork fat (not bacon, and nothing smoked, salted, or flavored), and if he'll dice it for you, great. You'll need about a pound of fat for a cup of lard. Put the cubes into a big Dutch oven and cook over medium-low heat for about 45 minutes. The fat will melt, leaving you with crispy little snacks for you and/or your dog. When the pan is cool enough for you to handle, pour the liquid through a fine sieve or several layers of cheesecloth. Store the lard for several weeks in a resealable plastic container in the refrigerator.

Butter gives a wonderful flavor to some dessert tamales. The recipes in this book always call for unsalted butter.

Shortening may be the only acceptable option for some people, including strict vegetarians. If you absolutely cannot use lard or butter, try using solid palm oil, which is slightly less bad for you than partially hydrogenated vegetable oil (such as Crisco).

Avocados are native to Central America. Choose the smaller, bumpy-surfaced Hass variety over the bland, smooth-skinned Florida avocados. They will almost always need a few days to ripen on the counter.

OTHER INGREDIENTS

Banana leaves can be found frozen in Latin American and Asian markets, as well as online. The leaves lend a distinctive, appealing aroma to the masa as the tamales cook. Allow the leaves to defrost at room temperature before cutting them to about 6 by 8 inches with kitchen shears, removing the thick central rib. Soften the pieces over the flame of your range or grill. Remember that masa is always spread on the smooth side of the banana leaf.

Canela, also known as Mexican cinnamon or Ceylon cinnamon, is different from the tropical evergreen bark that Americans are used to, which is known as cassia cinnamon. Usually sold in "stick" form, canela is much thinner-skinned, mild, and sweet. Once you taste it, you won't want to go back to the thick, harsh cassia cinnamon. You can grind canela in a spice grinder or clean coffee grinder.

Chocolate. In Mexico, drinking chocolate is flavored with cinnamon or canela, and often almond or vanilla. It is pressed into tablets that are often used for cooking (as in mole). Look for brands like Nestlé's Abuelita or Ibarra in the ethnic foods section of your grocery store.

Cilantro is related to parsley, dill, chervil, and fennel, but it is much more controversial than any other herb—people tend to either love it or hate it. The bright, fresh, citrusy flavor is absolutely essential to Mexican and Latin American cuisines.

Coriander seed comes from the cilantro plant. You can toast the seeds briefly in a hot, dry skillet before grinding them in a spice grinder or clean coffee grinder.

Corn husks (dried) are found in many grocery stores and Latin American markets. Look for large, well-cleaned husks.

Garlic, like its cousins the onion, leek, shallot, and chive, is a member of the lily family. Mexican garlic has streaks of violet marking its papery bulbs and a somewhat milder flavor than American garlic. Do not buy jars of garlic; the flavor is nothing like fresh.

Huitlacoche (also spelled *cuitlacoche*) is a fungus (*Ustilago maydis*) that grows naturally on ears of corn. The fungus is harvested and regarded as a delicacy. The earthy and some-what smoky fungus is used to flavor quesadillas, tamales, soups, and other specialty dishes.

Mexican oregano has a very different flavor from Mediter-ranean oregano. If you use Mediterranean oregano, whatever you make will remind you of spaghetti sauce. Don't do it. Look for Mexican oregano in the spice aisle or in the Mexican or eth-nic foods section of your grocery store.

Onions. White onions are the standard in Mexico, where they are prized for their clean, sweet, tangy flavor.

Piñon. In Italy, these nuts are called *pignolia;* you may also know them as pine nuts. The piñons of Mexico and the Amer-ican Southwest come from a different species of pine tree, and the nuts have a slightly different flavor. These high-fat nuts are gathered by hand and may be expensive, but their distinctive flavor is a pleasure. For added flavor, briefly roast shelled piñons in a hot, dry skillet.

Stock or broth is always best when homemade and unsalted. If you use store-bought stock, choose a high-quality, low-sodium brand like Swanson's Natural Goodness. Once you choose a brand of store-bought stock, stick with it; once you get used to it you'll notice the difference in flavor if you try another.

Tomatillos are related to tomatoes (and also to gooseberries, hence their common papery husks) and are much more popular in Mexico than in the U.S. Known south of the border as *tomates verdes,* they may cause translation problems, but you'll have no problem telling the difference. Tomatillos have a unique tart flavor that is *almost* like unripe tomatoes, but much brighter and more citrusy. Fresh tomatillos are firm, with soft husks that cling to the fruit. Roasting tomatillos in a cast-iron skillet or on the grill mellows their flavor.

Tomatoes. Always let tomatoes ripen on the counter. Never refrigerate them unless they're about to go bad and you need to save them for one more day. Roasting them will add a more complex flavor. You can roast tomatoes in a cast-iron skillet, under a broiler, or on a grill.

CHILES Chiles provide the kick that keeps us addicted to salsa. More and more varieties of chiles show up every day in American supermarkets, and you'll likely find a surprising array of chiles for sale at your local farmers market (also see "Sources," page 86). Don't be afraid to substitute one chile for another. It may be untraditional, but your experiments will always be interesting (and almost always edible). Just remember to add a little bit at a time.

Amarillo is the generic term for dried yellow chiles in Mexico, but most commonly they are chilcostles or chilhuacles. Use any dried yellow chile you can find.

Anchos are dried poblano chiles. They are broad-shouldered, with a dark red color and mild, raisiny flavor.

Chile Caribe is the term used to describe crushed red New Mexico chile pods that are often used as a garnish or made into a chile paste. Chile Caribe has a fruity, medium-hot flavor.

Chipotle chiles are smoked jalapeños with an intense smoky flavor and sharp heat. They are commonly available canned, in a tomato-based adobo sauce. Dried chipotles come in two main varieties: the shiny, dark red variety called *morita*, and a dull, leathery-looking form called *meco*. Use whatever you can get your hands on.

De árbol chiles are skinny little red chiles most often found dried. They are quite hot.

Guajillos are bright red chiles that resemble dried red New Mexico chiles, but their skins are far tougher, and they must be soaked in hot water longer before they soften. They are quite hot, but very flavorful.

Jalapeños are short, dark green, and hot, with a fresh, tart flavor. Pickled jalapeños are slightly milder and are often used as a garnish.

New Mexico red chiles are big, long, dried red chiles. Thin-skinned with a bright, fruity flavor, they are some of the most common red chiles in grocery stores.

Pasillas are long, skinny, dark brown chiles with a medium-hot kick and a rich, complex flavor. They are also sometimes called *chiles negros.*

Pequín chiles are tiny (or *pequeño,* in Spanish) but incredibly fiery. They are commonly crushed between the fingers and sprinkled into dishes.

Poblanos, the fresh form of anchos, are heart-shaped, dark green chiles with a mild heat. They have a much more complex flavor than green bell peppers and taste wonderful when roasted (see page 33).

Serranos, native to the mountains north of Puebla, Mexico, are small, dark green chiles that look like skinny jalapeños. Like jalapeños, they are quite hot, with a fresh, citrusy flavor.

EQUIPMENT *Cast-iron skillet.* A large, cast-iron skillet, which becomes nonstick with use and age, is very useful for toasting spices, heating tortillas, and frying meats.

Standing mixer. Sure, you can make tamale dough by hand, but you'll find that a standing electric mixer saves an awful lot of elbow grease. It will also free up your hands for other tasks while the dough is being mixed.

Tamalera. To steam a small batch of tamales you can use a Chinese bamboo steamer or Thai aluminum steamer. Alternatively, you can make do by using a big stockpot or canning pot with a collapsible steamer rack in the bottom. But if you come across a big aluminum or galvanized metal tamalera, buy it. It will accommodate many, many more tamales at once.

Making Masa

xxxxxx

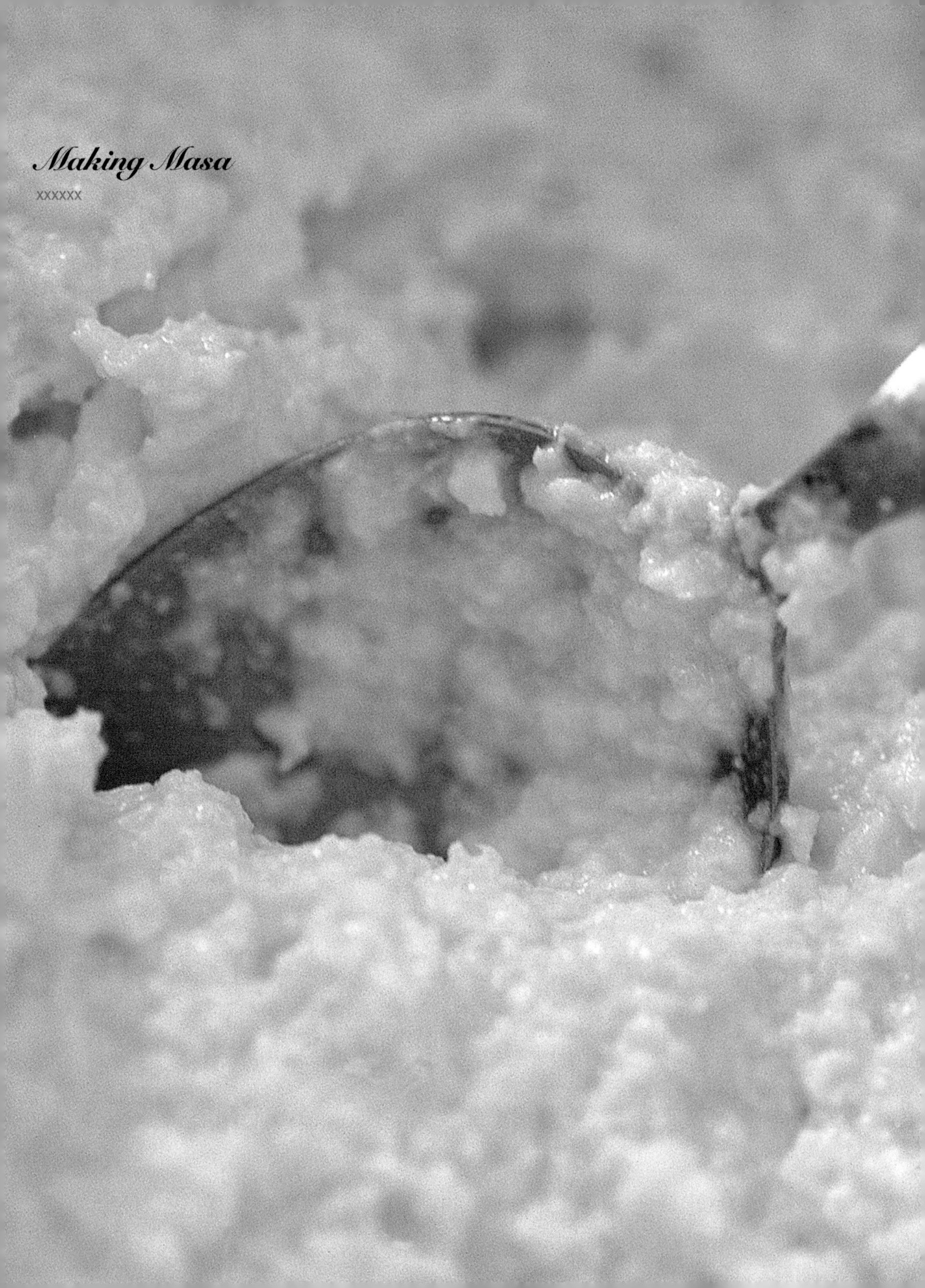

Basic Masa

xxxxxx

If you live near a tortillería *or a large Latin American grocery store, you may be able to buy moist, freshly ground masa, which is ideal for making tamales. Be sure to ask for* masa para tamales *that has not already been mixed with lard or shortening, and find out whether or not it has already been salted. If so, omit the salt in the recipe. (If the store renders their own lard, buy some of that, too!) Otherwise, you can make your own dough at home using masa harina and water.*

If you're using masa harina, pour it into a bowl and add 2 cups warm water. Work the mixture into a dough with your hands, then set it aside to rest for about 15 minutes.

Add the lard to the workbowl of a standing mixer fixed with the whisk attachment (or use a regular hand mixer in a large bowl) and beat it together with the salt and baking powder until light and fluffy.

If you're using a standing mixer, switch to the paddle attachment. While beating, add the reconstituted or fresh masa by handfuls into the workbowl. Add the stock and beat until combined. Taste the mixture and add salt if necessary.

Continue beating until the masa is light and fluffy, 15 to 20 minutes. The masa is ready when a grape-sized ball of dough floats in a glass of cold water. If the dough sinks, continue beating 5 minutes longer, then test it again.

Makes enough for about 24 medium tamales

2 pounds freshly ground masa for tamales, or 3 cups masa harina mixed with 2 cups warm water

1 cup fresh lard, at room temperature

1 1/2 teaspoons salt (or to taste)

1 1/2 teaspoons baking powder

1 1/2 cups homemade or low-sodium chicken stock

Heart-Smart Masa

xxxxxx

Makes enough for about 24 large tamales

6 cups masa harina

6 cups homemade or low-sodium chicken stock

1 cup canola oil

2 teaspoons salt

1½ teaspoons baking powder

This recipe, which I have adapted only slightly, was used in 2000 to make the tamale that won an award for the Best Commercial Gourmet Tamale at the International Tamale Festival in Indio, California (the winning recipe came from the makers of Maseca dried masa). If you've grown up on regular tamales, you'll definitely notice the difference, but if you're new to the genre, you might never guess it's made with canola oil.

In the workbowl of a standing mixer, beat together the masa harina, chicken stock, oil, salt, and baking powder until fully combined.

Fat-Free Masa

xxxxxx

Makes enough for about 12 medium tamales

3 cups masa harina

1 cup warm water

1 cup salsa

Yes, you can make tamales without any fat. The result may not have the same satisfying "oomph," but it's an interesting experiment. Try using this masa in any of the recipes in this book.

In the workbowl of a standing mixer, beat together the masa harina and water for 5 minutes. Add the salsa and beat for 1 more minute.

Vegetarian Masa

xxxxxx

Although I think lard gives the best results for tamales, you can also make a perfectly acceptable version using palm oil or vegetable shortening. Under no circumstances should you try to use margarine for tamales; it simply will not work. Look for solid palm oil and other trans-fat-free shortenings at your natural foods store.

If you're using masa harina, pour it into a bowl and add the 2 cups of warm water. Work the mixture into a dough with your hands, then set it aside to rest for about 15 minutes.

Add the palm oil or shortening to the workbowl of a standing mixer fixed with the whisk attachment (or use a regular hand mixer in a large bowl) and beat it together with the salt and baking powder until light and fluffy.

If you're using a standing mixer, switch to the paddle attachment. While beating, add the reconstituted or fresh masa by handfuls into the workbowl. Add the stock and beat until combined. Taste the mixture and add salt if necessary.

Continue beating until the masa is light and fluffy, about 15 or 20 minutes. The masa is ready when a grape-sized ball of dough floats in a glass of cold water. If the dough sinks, continue beating 5 minutes longer, then test it again.

Makes enough for about 24 medium tamales

2 pounds freshly ground masa for tamales, or 3 cups masa harina mixed with 2 cups warm water

1 cup solid palm oil or vegetable shortening

1 1/2 teaspoons salt (or to taste)

1 1/2 teaspoons baking powder

1 1/2 cups homemade or low-sodium vegetable stock

Blue Corn Masa

xxxxxx

Makes enough for about 12 large tamales

2 cups coarse blue cornmeal

1 teaspoon salt

2 cups homemade or low-sodium chicken broth

⅓ cup fresh lard, at room temperature

Blue corn tamales are rare, but beautiful. This quick and easy recipe is made with blue cornmeal. You can also use blue corn atole (finely ground cornmeal) or blue corn masa harina (flour) for this recipe, producing variations on texture. See "Sources," page 86, for where to find these products.

In a medium bowl, mix together the blue cornmeal and salt. Slowly add the broth, stirring with a fork until the mixture holds together.

Add the lard to the workbowl of a standing mixer fixed with the paddle attachment. Beat on low, adding the cornmeal mixture by the handful.

The masa is ready when a grape-sized ball of dough floats in a glass of cold water. If the dough sinks, continue beating 5 minutes longer, then test it again.

Pumpkin Masa

xxxxxx

Makes enough for about 24 small tamales

2 pounds freshly ground masa for tamales, or 3 cups masa harina plus 2 cups water

1/2 cup fresh lard, at room temperature

2 teaspoons salt (or to taste)

1 1/2 teaspoons baking powder

2 teaspoons coriander seed, toasted and ground (see page 14)

1 cup homemade or low-sodium chicken stock

1 cup cooked and pureed winter squash, or canned pumpkin

If you add a few tablespoons of sugar to this masa, it can be used for delightful sweet tamales. (And no, the chicken stock/sugar combination is not weird.)

If you're using masa harina, pour it into a bowl and add the water. Work the mixture into a dough with your hands, then set it aside to rest for about 15 minutes.

Add the lard to the workbowl of a standing mixer fixed with the whisk attachment (or use a regular hand mixer in a large bowl) and beat it together with the salt, baking powder, and coriander seed until light and fluffy.

If you're using a standing mixer, switch to the paddle attachment. While beating, add the reconstituted or fresh masa by handfuls into the workbowl. Add the stock and beat until combined. Taste the mixture and add salt if necessary.

Add the squash or pumpkin and continue beating until the masa is light and fluffy, about 15 or 20 minutes. The masa is ready when a grape-sized ball of dough floats in a glass of cold water. If the dough sinks, continue beating 5 minutes longer, then test it again.

Basic Sweet Masa

xxxxxx

With the addition of just a little cinnamon and some raisins, this dough is good to go, but its simple, sweet flavor makes an excellent base for all sorts of dessert tamales.

If you're using masa harina, pour it into a bowl and add the 1½ cups warm water. Work the mixture into a dough with your hands, then set it aside to rest for about 15 minutes.

Add the butter to the workbowl of a standing mixer fixed with the whisk attachment (or use a regular hand mixer in a large bowl) and beat it together with the salt, baking powder, and brown sugar until light and fluffy.

If you're using a standing mixer, switch to the paddle attachment. While beating, add the reconstituted or fresh masa by handfuls into the workbowl. Add the milk or water and beat until combined. Taste the mixture and add salt if necessary.

Continue beating until the masa is light and fluffy, 15 or 20 minutes. The masa is ready when a grape-sized ball of dough floats in a glass of cold water. If the dough sinks, continue beating 5 minutes longer, then test it again.

Makes enough for about 24 small tamales

$1\frac{1}{3}$ pounds freshly ground masa for tamales, or 2 cups masa harina mixed with $1\frac{1}{2}$ cups warm water

$2/3$ cup unsalted butter, at room temperature

1 teaspoon salt (or to taste)

1 teaspoon baking powder

$1/2$ cup brown sugar

2 cups milk or water

Rich, Sweet Masa

xxxxxx

Makes enough for about 24 small tamales

1 1/3 **pounds freshly ground masa for tamales, or 2 cups masa harina mixed with 1 1/2 cups warm water**

2/3 **cup lard or unsalted butter, at room temperature**

1 **teaspoon salt**

1 **can (14 ounces) sweetened condensed milk**

Salt (optional)

This recipe calls for sweetened condensed milk because its rich, sweet, almost caramelized flavor works well with the flavor of corn. Also, it seems like there's always a can of this stuff in the pantry, even when there's no milk in the fridge.

If you're using masa harina, pour it into a bowl and add the 1½ cups warm water. Work the mixture into a dough with your hands, then set it aside to rest for about 15 minutes.

Add the lard or butter to the workbowl of a standing mixer fixed with the whisk attachment (or use a regular hand mixer in a large bowl) and beat it together with the salt until light and fluffy.

If you're using a standing mixer, switch to the paddle attachment. While beating, add the reconstituted (or freshly ground) masa by handfuls into the workbowl. Add the milk and beat until combined. Taste the mixture and add salt if necessary.

Continue beating until the masa is light and fluffy, 15 or 20 minutes. The masa is ready when a grape-sized ball of dough floats in a glass of cold water. If the dough sinks, continue beating 5 minutes longer, then test it again.

Chocolate Masa

xxxxx

Just when you thought tamales couldn't get any better…

If you're using masa harina, pour it into a bowl and add the 1½ cups warm water. Work the mixture into a dough with your hands, then set it aside to rest for about 15 minutes.

In a small microwave-safe bowl, combine the chocolate chips and baking chocolate. Microwave on 50 percent power for 1½ minutes, then stir and repeat once or twice more until the chocolate is completely melted.

Add the butter to the workbowl of a standing mixer fixed with the whisk attachment (or use a regular hand mixer in a large bowl) and beat it together with the salt, baking powder, melted chocolate, brown sugar, vanilla, and canela or cinnamon until light and fluffy.

If you're using a standing mixer, switch to the paddle attachment. While beating, add the reconstituted or fresh masa by handfuls into the workbowl. Add the milk or water and beat until combined. Taste the mixture and add salt if necessary.

Continue beating until the masa is light and fluffy, 15 or 20 minutes. The masa is ready when a grape-sized ball of dough floats in a glass of cold water. If the dough sinks, continue beating 5 minutes longer, then test it again.

Makes enough for about 24 small tamales

1⅓ pounds freshly ground masa for tamales, or 2 cups masa harina mixed with 1½ cups warm water

1 cup bittersweet chocolate chips

2 squares (1 ounce apiece) unsweetened baking chocolate, coarsely chopped

½ cup unsalted butter, at room temperature

1 teaspoon salt

1 teaspoon baking powder

½ cup brown sugar

1 teaspoon vanilla extract

1 teaspoon freshly ground canela or ground cinnamon

2 cups milk or water

Salt (optional)

Coconut Masa

xxxxxx

Makes enough for about 24 small tamales

1 1/3 pounds freshly ground masa for tamales, or 2 cups masa harina mixed with 1 1/2 cups warm water

2/3 cup lard or unsalted butter, at room temperature

1 teaspoon salt

1/4 cup brown sugar

1 teaspoon vanilla extract

1 cup shredded coconut

1 can (13 ounces) coconut milk, plus enough water to make 2 cups

Salt (optional)

Don't use sweetened coconut flakes or the masa will become too sweet. Look for unsweetened shredded coconut in the bulk aisle at your natural foods store or in any Asian or Latin American market.

If you're using masa harina, pour it into a bowl and add 1½ cups warm water. Work the mixture into a dough with your hands, then set it aside to rest for about 15 minutes.

Add the lard or butter to the workbowl of a standing mixer fixed with the whisk attachment (or use a regular hand mixer in a large bowl) and beat it together with the salt until light and fluffy.

If you're using a standing mixer, switch to the paddle attachment. While beating, add the reconstituted (or freshly ground) masa by handfuls into the workbowl. Add the brown sugar, vanilla, shredded coconut, and coconut milk and water mixture, and beat until combined. Taste the mixture and add salt if necessary.

Continue beating until the masa is light and fluffy, 15 or 20 minutes. The masa is ready when a grape-sized ball of dough floats in a glass of cold water. If the dough sinks, continue beating 5 minutes longer, then test it again.

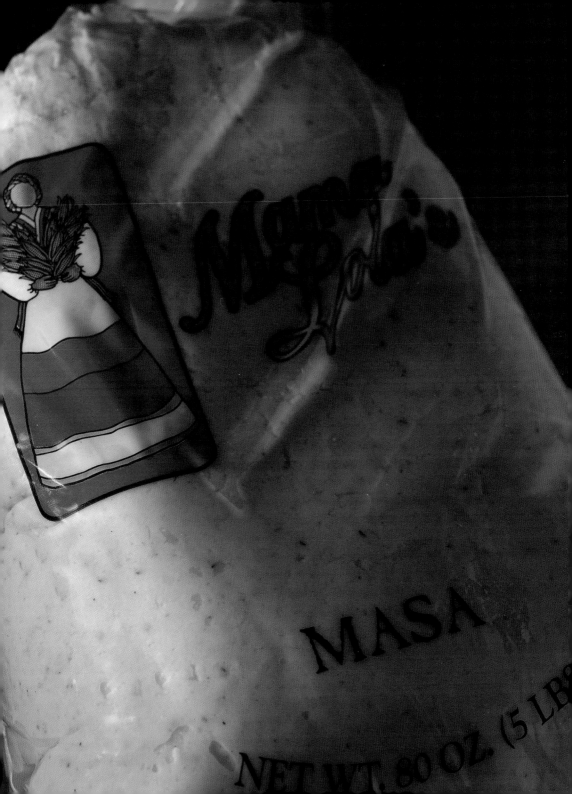

Savory Tamales

Summer Squash Tamales

xxxxxx

If you don't use all of this filling for your tamales, you can use some of it to stuff an omelet or mix it with some black beans for a quick burrito. For a slightly different flavor, you can substitute 2 poblanos or a handful of jalapeños for the New Mexico green chiles.

In a heavy skillet over medium-low heat, sauté the onion and garlic in the butter or vegetable oil until softened.

Meanwhile, cut the squash into 12 thick matchsticks, about ½ inch thick by 2½ inches long. Add the squash to the pan and cook, covered, about 10 minutes.

Slice the roasted chiles into strips about ½ inch wide and 2½ inches long.

In a medium-sized bowl, toss the chile strips and squash mixture to combine. Allow the mixture to cool to room temperature, then season to taste with salt.

To assemble the tamales, spread a few tablespoons of masa on a corn husk. Lay 1 piece of squash, 1 strip of green chile, and a few pieces of onion down the middle of the masa. Fold and tie; repeat with the remaining corn husks and ingredients.

Steam for 1 hour and serve plain or with Salsa Verde.

Makes 12 tamales

1 small white onion, sliced into half-moons

2 cloves garlic, minced

1 teaspoon butter or vegetable oil

1 medium summer squash (zucchini, crookneck, or pattypan)

2 fresh New Mexico green chiles, roasted, peeled, and seeded (directions follow)

Salt

$1/2$ recipe Vegetarian Masa (see page 23)

At least 16 softened corn husks, plus 16 strips for tying

Salsa Verde (optional, see page 73)

Roasting Chiles

xxxxxx

Over a gas flame, under a broiler, or on a grill, roast the chiles until they are dark and blistered. Place them in a bowl and cover with plastic wrap until they are cool enough to handle, about 15 minutes. Wearing latex disposable gloves, remove the stems, seeds, and charred skin from the chiles.

Green Corn Tamales with Green Chile

xxxxxx

Makes 12 tamales

10 ears fresh corn (or about 6 cups canned corn)

3 tablespoons unsalted butter

1/2 small white onion, diced

2 cloves garlic, minced

1 cup roasted, peeled, and chopped green chiles (see page 33, or use canned)

1/2 cup heavy cream

1/2 teaspoon baking powder

1/2 cup grits (uncooked)

Salt

16 softened corn husks, plus 16 strips for tying (if you're not using fresh corn)

Peach Salsa (see page 72), or salsa of your choice, for serving

This very traditional (except for the peach salsa) recipe is a celebration of summer. The light, airy masa is made with grits and, ideally, with fresh ears of corn. The green husks of the corn are used to wrap the tamales. If fresh corn is out of season, you can make a version that's almost as good with canned corn and dried husks. If you prefer a milder tamale, you can omit the green chiles. You can put a little cheese in the middle too, if you like.

If you are using fresh corn, remove the husks, discarding the silks, and set the husks aside.

Slice the corn kernels from the cobs, being careful to collect all of the juices.

In a large skillet over medium heat, melt the butter. Add the onion and garlic and sauté until softened. Add the green chiles, corn and its juices, and heavy cream; cook, stirring, about 5 minutes.

Remove the pan from the heat and stir in the baking powder and grits. Season to taste with salt.

Tear 16 strips from the fresh corn leaves, if you're using them.

To assemble the tamales, spread about ¼ cup filling in the middle of a corn leaf, then fold and tie it. Repeat for the remaining tamales.

Steam the tamales for 1 hour and serve plain, or with Peach Salsa or the salsa of your choice.

Blue Corn and Green Chile Tamales

xxxxxx

Makes 12 tamales

3 fresh New Mexico green chiles, roasted, peeled, and seeded (see page 33)

1 cup corn kernels

1/2 cup shredded Jack or Oaxaca cheese

1 recipe Blue Corn Masa (see page 24)

At least 16 softened corn husks, plus 16 strips for tying

New Mexico Green Chile Sauce (optional, see page 70)

Both blue corn and green chiles are native to the Southwest, although it is more common to find blue corn tortillas than blue corn tamales. The color of the cornmeal is actually closer to purple. Make these when you want something beautiful and unusual.

Coarsely chop the chiles. In a medium bowl, toss them with the corn and cheese.

To assemble the tamales, spread a few tablespoons of masa on a corn husk. Spread some of the filling down the center of the masa. Fold and tie; repeat with the remaining corn husks and ingredients.

Steam the tamales for 1 hour and serve plain or with New Mexico Green Chile Sauce.

Sweet Potato Tamales

xxxxxx

Try these sweet potato tamales alongside big, fat pork chops. If you substitute vegetable stock for the chicken stock, they make a nice vegetarian side dish. When you chop the chipotles in adobo, include whatever sauce clings to the chiles—no more, no less.

Preheat the oven to 350 degrees F. Bake the sweet potatoes for about 1 hour, or until cooked through. Allow the sweet potatoes to cool 20 minutes.

Pour the masa harina into a bowl and add the warm water. Work the mixture into a dough with your hands, then set it aside to rest for about 15 minutes.

Scoop the flesh from the sweet potatoes into the workbowl of a standing mixer; discard the skins. Add the butter, baking powder, chipotles, and maple syrup or honey to the workbowl and beat. Add the masa mixture in 3 parts, alternating with the chicken stock. Continue beating for about 10 minutes. Season to taste with salt.

To assemble the tamales, spread about ¼ cup of the filling mixture in the middle of a softened corn husk, then fold and tie it. Repeat for the remaining tamales.

Steam the tamales for 1 hour and serve hot.

Makes about 12 tamales

4 medium sweet potatoes

1 cup masa harina

$1/2$ cup warm water

$1/4$ cup unsalted butter, softened

1 teaspoon baking powder

2 chipotles in adobo, chopped

2 tablespoons maple syrup or honey

1 cup homemade or low-sodium chicken stock

Salt

At least 16 softened corn husks, plus 16 strips for tying

Grilled Trout Tamales with Sage and Bacon

xxxxxx

Makes 12 tamales

3 cups homemade or low-sodium vegetable stock

1 cup medium-grind cornmeal

2 teaspoons shredded fresh sage

3 strips cooked bacon, crumbled

Salt and freshly ground black pepper

At least 16 softened corn husks, plus 16 strips for tying

1 1/2 cups cooked trout, crumbled

New Mexico Green Chile Sauce (optional, see page 70)

My grandmother and I used to spend lazy afternoons fishing together at the pond on my grandparents' farm in Pennsylvania. Grandpa would clean the fish, and Grandma would wrap our catch in bacon and put them under the broiler. Make these easy tamales when you have some nice fresh-caught fish left over from dinner.

In a large stockpot, bring the stock to a boil. Sprinkle in the cornmeal while whisking constantly. Reduce heat to low and cook, stirring constantly with a whisk, then a spoon, for about 10 minutes, or until the mixture thickens and all of the water is absorbed.

Remove from the heat, stir in the sage and bacon, and season to taste with salt and pepper.

To assemble the tamales, spread about ¼ cup of the cornmeal mixture onto a corn husk. Spoon a couple of tablespoons of fish down the center of the masa. Fold and tie; repeat with the remaining corn husks and ingredients.

Preheat a gas or charcoal grill to medium high.

Place the tamales on a clean, oiled grill grate and cook for about 3 minutes on each side.

Serve plain or with New Mexico Green Chile Sauce.

Huitlacoche and Squash Blossom Tamales with Roasted Corn

xxxxxx

If it's not overkill to put a slab of foie gras on top of a piece of filet mignon, then it's not too decadent to put these two ingredients together in one dish. Huitlacoche, also known as corn smut, has a delightfully earthy flavor that is strangely alluring. It's not pretty, though—fortunately, the squash blossoms make these tamales as beautiful as they are delicious. Look for fresh squash blossoms at farmers markets or specialty food stores. If you happen to have some Black Mole (see page 74) on hand, a dab of it makes a nice accompaniment to these tamales.

Makes 12 tamales

2 ears fresh corn, shucked

1 tablespoon lard or unsalted butter

3 cloves garlic, minced

$1/2$ small white onion, finely chopped

2 cans ($7 1/2$ ounces each) huitlacoche

Salt and freshly ground black pepper

$1/2$ recipe Basic Masa (see page 21)

At least 16 softened corn husks, plus 16 strips for tying

12 fresh squash blossoms

Preheat a gas or charcoal grill to medium-high heat. Grill the corn, turning frequently, until it turns mostly golden with a few blackened spots. Turn off the grill and allow the corn to cool.

In a skillet over medium heat, melt the lard or butter. Sauté the garlic and onion until softened. Add the huitlacoche, reduce heat, and cook about 10 minutes, stirring frequently, until the mixture is thickened. Remove it from the heat, transfer to a blender or food processor, and puree.

Cut the roasted corn kernels from the cob and transfer them to a medium bowl. Add the huitlacoche mixture and toss to combine. Season to taste with salt and pepper.

In the workbowl of a standing mixer, beat together the Basic Masa and the huitlacoche mixture.

Trim the stems from the squash blossoms and gently open them to check for insects; if you find any, shoo them away. Note: you can't really rinse the blossoms—they are too delicate.

To assemble the tamales, spread ⅓ to ½ cup of masa on a corn husk. Lift the long sides of the husk together towards the middle, pressing the masa into a log. Drop the sides of the husk. Gently press a squash blossom into the top surface of the tamale, then fold and tie. Repeat with the remaining corn husks and ingredients.

Steam the tamales for 1 hour and serve warm.

Shredded Pork Tamales

xxxxx

*Makes about
12 tamales*

1 recipe New Mexico Red
Chile Sauce (see page 69)

¹/₂ recipe Basic Masa
(see page 21)

At least 16 softened
corn husks, plus 16
strips for tying

1¹/₂ cups shredded
cooked pork

For this recipe you can use any kind of leftover shredded pork. Pulled pork, like you'd get at a barbecue restaurant, is fine just as long as it has no sauce on it.

In the workbowl of a standing mixer, beat ½ cup of the red chile sauce into the masa.

To assemble the tamales, spread a few tablespoons of masa on a corn husk. Arrange a few spoonfuls of shredded pork down the middle of the masa. Fold and tie; repeat with the remaining corn husks and ingredients.

Steam for 1 hour and serve with the remaining New Mexico Red Chile Sauce.

Pumpkin Raisin Tamales with Shredded Beef

xxxxxx

This recipe will unnerve people who don't like mixing sweet and savory in the same dish (and believe me, they're out there). But I think it's absolutely fantastic. I have adapted it from a recipe developed by chef Pilar Sanchez as a showcase for California raisins.

Place the beef and onion in a large stockpot and add enough cold water to cover. Bring the water to a boil over high heat, then reduce the heat, cover, and simmer for about 1½ hours. Remove the beef from the broth and let rest for 10 minutes; reserve the broth. Using two forks, shred the beef, discarding any excess fat.

Add the olive oil to a large skillet set over medium heat and sauté the carrots and celery for 5 minutes. Stir in the shredded beef and raisins, along with 1 cup of the reserved broth. Reduce the heat to low and simmer for 5 minutes. Season to taste with salt and pepper and allow the mixture to cool completely.

To assemble the tamales, spread about ⅓ cup pumpkin masa onto the center of each corn husk. Spoon about ¼ cup of the shredded beef filling down the center of the dough. Fold and tie the tamale; repeat with the remaining ingredients and husks.

Steam the tamales for 1½ hours and serve plain or with New Mexico Red Chile Sauce.

Makes 12 large tamales

2 pounds boneless beef chuck or shoulder

1 onion, peeled and halved

Water

¼ cup olive oil

1 cup finely chopped carrots

1 cup finely chopped celery

1 cup California raisins

Salt and freshly ground black pepper

1 recipe Pumpkin Masa (see page 26)

At least 16 softened corn husks, plus 16 strips for tying

New Mexico Red Chile Sauce (optional, see page 69)

Pork and Red Chile Tamales

xxxxxx

Makes about 24 tamales

2½ pounds boneless pork butt, trimmed of excess fat

6 cloves garlic, peeled

1 teaspoon black peppercorns

2 bay leaves

1 teaspoon salt

Water

1 recipe New Mexico Red Chile Sauce (see page 69)

1 recipe Basic Masa (see page 21) or Heart Smart Masa (see page 22)

At least 36 softened corn husks, plus 36 strips for tying

These are some of the most common tamales in the Southwest. They can be found in restaurants, cafés, and in the coolers toted by strolling vendors. Everybody loves them, so make a bunch and freeze any leftovers. This recipe makes enough pork filling to make another batch of tamales, but you can always just use the extra pork for burritos or freeze it for later use. I've heard that in some families it's traditional to put a single stuffed green olive in each of these tamales.

Arrange the pork butt in a large Dutch oven or heavy-bottomed stockpot. Add the garlic, peppercorns, bay leaves, and salt. Add enough cold water to cover by several inches. Bring the liquid to a boil, then reduce the heat and simmer, partially covered, for about 2 hours.

Transfer the pork to a cutting board and allow it to rest 20 minutes. Using two forks, shred the meat. In a bowl, combine 2 cups of the shredded pork with enough New Mexico Red Chile Sauce to thoroughly moisten the meat.

To assemble the tamales, spread about ⅓ cup masa onto the center of each corn husk. Spoon some of the shredded pork filling down the center of the dough. Fold and tie the tamale; repeat with the remaining ingredients and husks.

Steam the tamales for 1 hour and serve slathered with the remaining New Mexico Red Chile Sauce.

Green Chile Chicken Tamales

xxxxxx

This is an extremely flexible recipe. You'll need about 2 cups of shredded chicken, but it doesn't really matter where you get it—use grilled boneless skinless breasts, broiled thighs, or just pickings from a store-bought rotisserie chicken (one without any fancy seasonings, please). This recipe can easily be doubled or tripled. If you really like to slather your tamales with sauce, you should make a double batch of whichever sauce or salsa you choose.

In a large bowl, combine the chicken and either the chile sauce, salsa, or guacamole. Stir in the oregano, and add salt and pepper to taste.

To assemble the tamales, spread about ⅓ cup of masa onto the center of each corn husk. Spoon some of the shredded chicken filling down the center of the dough. Fold and tie the tamale; repeat with the remaining ingredients and corn husks.

Steam the tamales for 1 hour and serve with the remaining New Mexico Green Chile Sauce, Salsa Verde, or Guacamole Sauce.

Makes about 24 tamales

2 cups shredded cooked chicken

1 recipe New Mexico Green Chile Sauce (see page 70), Salsa Verde (see page 73), or Guacamole Sauce (see page 70)

2 teaspoons Mexican oregano

Salt and freshly ground black pepper

1 recipe Basic Masa (see page 21) or Heart-Smart Masa (see page 22)

At least 36 softened corn husks, plus 36 strips for tying

Tamales de Mole Amarillo

xxxxxx

*Makes about
12 tamales*

1 1/2 cups shredded cooked
chicken or pork (see
Pork and Red Chile
Tamales, page 42)

1 recipe Mole Amarillo
(see page 76)

Salt and freshly
ground black pepper

1/2 recipe Basic Masa (see
page 21) or Heart-Smart
Masa (see page 22)

At least 16 softened
corn husks, plus 16
strips for tying

12 sprigs fresh cilantro

Peach Salsa
(optional, see page 72)

*Sometimes I like to crumble these tamales into a bowl of Mole
Amarillo sauce and eat them with a spoon.*

In a large bowl, combine the chicken or pork and the Mole
Amarillo. Add salt and pepper to taste.

To assemble the tamales, spread about 1/3 cup masa onto the
center of each corn husk. Spoon some of the shredded meat
filling down the center of the dough. Top it with a sprig of
cilantro, then fold and tie the tamale; repeat with the remaining ingredients and husks.

Steam the tamales for 1 hour and serve with the remaining
Mole Amarillo or with Peach Salsa.

Wild Mushroom and Asparagus Tamales

xxxxxx

These tamales are the perfect way to celebrate the coming of spring.

In a cast-iron skillet over medium heat, melt the butter. Add the shallots and sauté until translucent. Add the mushrooms and asparagus and cook, stirring, for 2 minutes. Add the stock and wait for it to come to a boil, then reduce the heat and simmer about 5 minutes, or until the asparagus is just tender. Remove from the heat and season to taste with salt and pepper.

To assemble the tamales, spread about ⅓ cup of the prepared masa onto the center of a corn husk. Spoon some of the mushroom filling down the center of the dough. Top it with 1 or 2 pieces of asparagus, then fold and tie the tamale; repeat with the remaining ingredients and husks.

Steam the tamales for 1 hour and serve plain or with dollops of sour cream and/or Guacamole Sauce, if you like.

Makes about 12 tamales

$^1/_4$ cup unsalted butter

2 shallots, minced

$^1/_2$ pound fresh morels and/or other wild mushrooms, coarsely chopped

$^1/_2$ pound asparagus, cut into 2-inch-long pieces

$^1/_4$ cup homemade or low-sodium vegetable stock

Salt and freshly ground pepper

$^1/_2$ recipe Basic Masa (see page 21) or Vegetarian Masa (see page 23)

At least 16 softened corn husks, plus 16 strips for tying

Sour cream, for garnish (optional)

1 recipe Guacamole Sauce, for garnish (optional, see page 70)

Oaxacan Tamales with Mole Negro

xxxxxx

*Makes about
12 tamales*

1 recipe Black Mole
(see page 74)

1/2 recipe Heart-Smart
Masa (see page 22)

1 1/2 cups shredded
cooked turkey

1/2 cup dried cranberries
(optional)

Salt and freshly
ground black pepper

At least 16 softened
corn husks, plus
16 strips for tying

Wondering what to do with all that leftover turkey on the third Friday in November? Here's your answer. I love these with dried cranberries, but if you think that's just too weird, you can leave them out.

In a large bowl, pour ½ cup Black Mole over the masa and work it into the dough.

In another bowl, combine the turkey with enough mole to moisten it, and dried cranberries. Add salt and pepper to taste.

To assemble the tamales, spread about ⅓ cup of the masa mixture onto the center of a corn husk. Spoon some of the shredded turkey filling down the center of the dough. Fold and tie the tamale; repeat with the remaining ingredients and corn husks.

Steam the tamales for 1 hour and serve with the remaining Mole Negro.

Humitas

xxxxxx

Makes about 12 humitas

12 ears fresh corn

1/4 cup masa harina

2 tablespoons warm water

1/4 cup unsalted butter

1 medium white onion, diced

3 cloves garlic, minced

1 tablespoon paprika

1/4 cup chopped fresh basil

Salt

Smoky Chipotle Salsa Roja (optional, see page 73)

The humita *is a South American cousin to the tamales of Mexico and Central America. Make them when you can get good fresh corn. If you'd like a spicier humita, substitute chile powder for some of the paprika.*

Remove the husks from the corn, discarding the silks, and set the husks aside.

In a small bowl, combine the masa harina with the warm water.

Slice the corn kernels from the cobs, being careful to collect all of the juices. Puree the kernels and their juices in a food processor or blender.

In a large skillet over medium heat, melt the butter. Add the onion and garlic and sauté until softened. Add the pureed corn and cook, stirring, about 5 minutes. Add the masa harina mixture and paprika, and cook 10 minutes longer. Stir in the basil and remove from the heat. Add salt to taste.

To assemble the tamales, spread about ¼ cup filling in the middle of a fresh green corn husk, then fold and tie it. Repeat for the remaining tamales.

Steam the tamales for 1 hour and serve with Smoky Chipotle Salsa Roja or the salsa of your choice.

Red Chile Bison Tamale Pie

xxxxxx

Bison meat is becoming more and more common in the West as supply starts to catch up with demand for this low-fat, high-protein meat.

Preheat oven to 350 degrees F.

In a large skillet, sauté the onion and garlic in the lard or oil until just translucent. Add the ground bison and brown the meat on all sides. Add the New Mexico Red Chile Sauce, reduce the heat, and simmer for 20 minutes.

Meanwhile, bring 2 cups of the stock to a boil. In a small bowl, mix the salt and cornmeal with the remaining 2 cups of stock. Pour the cornmeal mixture into the boiling stock and whisk to combine. Cook and stir for 5 minutes. Remove from heat and cover.

Grease a 9 x 13-inch baking dish and press half of the cornmeal mixture into it. Top with the ground bison mixture and sliced olives. Top with the other half of the cornmeal mixture.

Bake for 20 minutes or until golden.

Serves 6

1 small white onion, chopped

2 cloves garlic, minced

l tablespoon lard or vegetable oil

1 pound ground bison

1½ cups New Mexico Red Chile Sauce (see page 69)

4 cups homemade or low-sodium beef stock

1 teaspoon salt

1 cup cornmeal

¼ cup sliced green olives

Ratatouille Tamales

xxxxxx

Makes about 24 tamales

1 medium zucchini, diced

1 medium eggplant, peeled and diced

1 yellow bell pepper, seeded and diced

1 red bell pepper, seeded and diced

$1/2$ pint cherry tomatoes, halved

1 medium yellow onion, diced

6 cloves garlic, peeled

$1/2$ cup extra-virgin olive oil

Salt and freshly ground black pepper

$1/2$ cup chopped cilantro

1 recipe Vegetarian Masa (see page 23)

At least 36 softened corn husks, plus 36 strips for tying

Smoky Chipotle Salsa Roja (optional, see page 73)

This is one way to get them to eat their vegetables.

Preheat oven to 400 degrees F.

In a large bowl, toss the zucchini, eggplant, yellow and red bell peppers, tomatoes, onion, and garlic with the olive oil and sprinkle them with salt and pepper. Transfer them to a large roasting pan and bake for 1 hour. Remove the pan from the heat and allow it to cool completely before stirring in the cilantro.

To assemble the tamales, spread a few tablespoons of the Vegetarian Masa on a corn husk. Spoon some of the vegetable mixture down the middle of the masa. Fold and tie; repeat with the remaining corn husks and ingredients.

Steam for 1 hour and serve plain or with Smoky Chipotle Salsa Roja.

Lamb Tamales with Piñon Nuts and Mint

xxxxxx

These tamales are also very good when made without the ground lamb, but served alongside a lamb chop.

In a large skillet over medium-high heat, heat the olive oil and sauté the onion and garlic until translucent. Add the lamb and brown on all sides. Add the cinnamon, cumin, piñons, and paprika or red chile powder, and stir to combine. Remove from the heat and season to taste with salt and pepper.

In a large bowl, work the fresh mint into the masa.

To assemble the tamales, spread ⅓ to ½ cup of masa on a corn husk. Spoon a few spoonfuls of the lamb mixture down the middle of the masa. Fold and tie; repeat with the remaining corn husks and ingredients.

Steam the tamales for 1 hour and serve with a sauce of plain yogurt thinned with a little lemon juice, to taste.

Makes about 12 tamales

1 tablespoon olive oil

1 small white onion, finely chopped

2 cloves garlic, finely minced

½ pound ground lamb

½ teaspoon ground cinnamon

2 teaspoons ground cumin

⅓ cup toasted piñon nuts

2 teaspoons paprika or red chile powder

Salt and freshly ground black pepper

¼ cup finely chopped mint leaves

½ recipe Basic Masa (see page 21)

At least 16 softened corn husks, plus 16 strips for tying

2 cups plain yogurt, for serving

Lemon juice, for serving

Salmon Tamales with Peach Salsa

xxxxxx

Makes 12 tamales

3 cups homemade or low-sodium vegetable stock

1 cup medium-grind cornmeal

Grated zest of 1 lemon

Salt and freshly ground black pepper

At least 12 pieces banana leaf (each 6 x 8 inches), plus strips for tying

1 pound barely cooked salmon, cut into strips

1 recipe Peach Salsa (see page 72)

This light, fruity salsa is the perfect foil for the rich, full flavor of salmon. If you're feeling adventurous, you might also try these tamales made with unsweetened Coconut Masa (see page 30), omitting the steps listed in this recipe for the vegetable stock, cornmeal, lemon zest, and salt and pepper.

In a large stockpot, bring the stock to a boil. Sprinkle in the cornmeal while whisking constantly. Reduce heat to low and cook, stirring constantly with a whisk, then a spoon, for about 10 minutes, or until the mixture thickens and all of the water is absorbed.

Remove from the heat, stir in the zest, and season to taste with salt and pepper.

To assemble the tamales, spread about ¼ cup of the cornmeal mixture onto a banana leaf. Arrange one strip of salmon down the center of the masa. Fold and tie; repeat with the remaining banana leaves and ingredients.

Steam the tamales for 45 minutes, or grill as for Grilled Trout Tamales with Sage and Bacon (see page 38). Serve with Peach Salsa.

Maple-Flavored Breakfast Tamales

xxxxxx

Really, you can put anything you want in a tamale. Hard-boiled eggs are not uncommon, so why not throw in some bacon or sausage and call it breakfast?

In the workbowl of a standing mixer, beat the maple syrup into the masa. Season to taste with black pepper.

To assemble the tamales, spread a few tablespoons of masa on a corn husk. Arrange half a piece of bacon or sausage link and 2 pieces of egg down the middle of the masa. Fold and tie; repeat with the remaining corn husks and ingredients.

Steam for 1 hour and serve with coffee and the morning paper.

Makes about 12 tamales

$1/3$ cup maple syrup

$1/2$ recipe Basic Masa (see page 21)

Freshly ground black pepper

At least 16 softened corn husks, plus 16 strips for tying

6 pieces cooked bacon, or 6 breakfast sausage links, halved

6 hard-boiled eggs, peeled and quartered lengthwise

Sweet Tamales

xxxxxx

No-Masa Fresh Corn Tamales

xxxxxx

These special tamales can be made only with fresh corn on the cob—preferably field corn, which we don't usually see in grocery stores. Look for it at farmers markets. Once you've pureed the corn, it's hard to imagine that the messy, pudding-like filling will ever firm up, but somehow it works. The result is very light, delicate, and wonderful. If you add enough sugar, plus a little cinnamon and maybe a few raisins, these can easily become dessert tamales.

Makes about 12 tamales

12 ears fresh corn

1 1/2 cups brown sugar

1 1/2 cups corn oil

Salt

Cut the bottoms from the corn cobs to free the husks, and carefully peel them away. Reserve the husks, but discard the silk.

Cut the kernels from the cobs and place them in the workbowl of a food processor or blender. With the motor running, add the brown sugar. Pour the corn oil into the workbowl in a thin stream. Add salt to taste.

To assemble the tamales, spoon about ½ cup of the filling into the center of each corn husk. Wrap and tie the tamale with a strip of corn husk; repeat with the remaining ingredients and corn husks.

Steam the tamales for 1 hour, then allow them to cool to room temperature before serving.

Chestnut Raisin Tamales

xxxxxx

*Makes about
12 tamales*

¹/₂ recipe Basic Sweet Masa
(see page 27)

¹/₃ cup golden raisins

¹/₃ cup sweetened chestnut
puree (see "Sources," 86)

¹/₄ teaspoon freshly
grated nutmeg

At least 16 softened
corn husks, plus 16
strips for tying

Whipped cream or
vanilla ice cream,
for serving

Sweetened chestnut puree is a French delicacy also known as crème de marrons. I happened to have some on hand one day when I was experimenting with sweet tamales, and I discovered that it makes a fabulous tamale flavoring.

Place the masa in a large bowl and work the raisins, chestnut puree, and nutmeg into the masa.

To assemble the tamales, spread about ⅓ cup of filling in the middle of a softened corn husk, then fold and tie it. Repeat for the remaining tamales.

Steam the tamales for 1 hour and serve hot with whipped cream or vanilla ice cream.

Indian Pudding Tamales

xxxxxx

After tasting some of my sweet tamales, my mother, who was raised in the Northeast, suggested I try Indian Pudding as a filling. Made with cornmeal, molasses, and ginger, and with a flavor much like gingerbread, Indian Pudding can be eaten for breakfast like a thick porridge, or baked like a casserole and served for dessert. Here I've thickened the pudding for a Northeast/Southwest hybrid tamale. Incidentally, the only fat in these tamales comes from the milk (if at all), so I suggest splurging on a big scoop of vanilla ice cream served over each one.

In a small saucepan over medium-high heat, bring the milk to a boil, then remove from the heat.

Set up a double boiler: Pour water to a depth of 3 inches into another saucepan and bring it to a simmer. Set a stainless steel bowl over the saucepan, making sure the bottom of the bowl does not touch the water below. If it does, pour out some water. Put the cornmeal and salt in the top of the double boiler and pour the hot milk over it, whisking constantly. Cook this mixture for about 15 minutes, whisking occasionally, until the cornmeal is thick and smooth. Remove it from the heat. Stir in the brown sugar, molasses, ginger, cinnamon, and raisins. Set the mixture aside and allow it to cool about 15 minutes.

To assemble the tamales, spread ¼ to ⅓ cup filling in the middle of a softened corn husk, then fold and tie the tamale. Repeat for the remaining tamales. Steam the tamales for 1 hour and serve warm with vanilla ice cream.

Makes about 12 tamales

2 cups milk

½ cup yellow or white cornmeal

½ teaspoon salt

¼ cup light-brown sugar

¼ cup molasses

½ teaspoon ground ginger

½ teaspoon ground cinnamon

½ cup raisins

At least 16 softened corn husks, plus 16 strips for tying

Vanilla ice cream, for serving

Baby Banana Tamales with Coconut and Brown Sugar

xxxxxx

Makes about 12 tamales

½ recipe Coconut Masa (see page 30)

½ cup unsweetened shredded coconut

1 teaspoon vanilla extract

⅓ cup brown sugar

At least 12 pieces of banana leaf (6 x 8 inches), plus more for tying

12 baby bananas, peeled

Vanilla ice cream, for serving

1 recipe Dulce de Leche (see page 78), for serving

I just happened to have a bunch of baby bananas sitting on the counter one day when inspiration struck, and now these are my absolute favorite tamales. The fun part is watching your guests' faces when they dig into the tamale and find a whole banana inside. Wrapping the tamales in banana leaves gives more flavor, but use corn husks if that's all you have.

Place the masa in a large bowl and work the shredded coconut, vanilla, and brown sugar into the masa.

To assemble the tamales, spread about ⅓ cup of filling in the middle of a softened piece of banana leaf, press a baby banana into the masa, then fold and tie it. Repeat for the remaining tamales.

Steam the tamales for 1 hour and serve hot with vanilla ice cream and Dulce de Leche.

Sweet Pumpkin Tamales

xxxxxx

*Makes about
12 tamales*

½ recipe Pumpkin
Masa (see page 26)

¼ cup molasses

½ cup brown sugar

⅓ cup evaporated milk

½ teaspoon ground
cinnamon

¼ teaspoon freshly
grated nutmeg

½ teaspoon ground ginger

1 pinch ground cloves

At least 16 softened
corn husks, plus 16
strips for tying

Vanilla ice cream,
for serving

1 recipe Dulce de Leche
(see page 78), for serving

These taste just like pumpkin pie! Well, sort of.

Place the masa in the workbowl of a standing mixer and beat in the molasses, brown sugar, evaporated milk, cinnamon, nutmeg, ginger, and cloves.

To assemble the tamales, spread ⅓ to ½ cup filling in the middle of a softened corn husk, then fold and tie it. Repeat for the remaining tamales.

Steam the tamales for 1 hour and serve hot with vanilla ice cream and Dulce de Leche.

Goat Cheese, Rosemary, and Fig Tamales

xxxxxx

These Mediterranean flavors combine in an interesting way with the Blue Corn Masa. I like to make these tamales in little ball shapes and wrap them up in little pouches.

Place the masa in a large bowl and work in the rosemary, goat cheese, and honey. Taste the masa and add more honey if needed.

Tear each corn husk in half.

To assemble the tamales, spread ⅓ to ½ cup of filling in a circle in the middle of a pair of criss-crossed softened corn husks, press a fig half into the masa, then fold the husks up around the masa and tie it. Repeat for the remaining tamales.

Steam the tamales for 1 hour and serve with Dulce de Leche on the side.

Makes about 12 tamales

1 recipe Blue Corn Masa (see page 24)

$1/2$ teaspoon minced fresh rosemary

$1/3$ cup fresh goat cheese

$1/2$ cup honey (or more)

At least 16 softened corn husks, plus 16 strips for tying

6 fresh Mission figs, halved

1 recipe Dulce de Leche (see page 78), for serving

Chocolate Tamales with Chile and Dried Cherries

xxxxxx

I used ancho chile powder for this recipe because I happened to have it handy. You can also use another pure ground chile powder (such as guajillo) or rehydrate a dried chile and chop it fine. Look for dried cherries in the bulk aisle at your favorite natural foods store, or in the fruit and nut aisle at better grocery stores.

Place the masa in a large bowl and work the dried cherries and ancho powder into the masa.

To assemble the tamales, spread about ⅓ cup filling in the middle of a softened corn husk, then fold and tie it. Repeat for the remaining tamales.

Steam the tamales for 1 hour and serve hot with vanilla ice cream and Dulce de Leche or Mexican Chocolate Ganache.

Makes about 12 tamales

½ recipe Chocolate Masa (see page 29)

½ cup dried cherries (sweet or sour), minced

1 tablespoon ancho chile powder

At least 16 softened corn husks, plus 16 strips for tying

Vanilla ice cream, for serving

1 recipe Dulce de Leche (see page 78) or Mexican Chocolate Ganache (see page 77), for serving

Sweet Tamales with Cinnamon and Anise

xxxxxx

Makes 12 tamales

½ recipe Rich, Sweet Masa (see page 28)

3 teaspoons anise seed

2 teaspoons freshly ground canela or ground cinnamon

At least 12 pieces banana leaf (6 x 8 inches each), plus strips for tying

Vanilla ice cream, for serving

1 recipe Dulce de Leche (see page 78) or Mexican Chocolate Ganache (see page 77), for serving

These tamales have a flavor reminiscent of Mexican wedding cookies.

Place the masa in a large bowl and work in the anise seed and canela or cinnamon.

To assemble the tamales, spread ⅓ to ½ cup filling in the middle of a softened piece of banana leaf, then fold and tie it. Repeat for the remaining tamales.

Steam the tamales for 1 hour and serve hot with vanilla ice cream and Dulce de Leche or Mexican Chocolate Ganache.

Sauces for Tamales

New Mexico Red Chile Sauce

XXXXXX

Here is my version of New Mexico's famous red chile sauce. Mixed with shredded pork, it is used as a tamale filling, but all by itself it is also ladled over tamales as well as enchiladas, huevos rancheros, breakfast burritos, stuffed sopaipillas, chiles rellenos, and almost anything else you can think of. You may not need 4 cups of the sauce for your recipe, but you might as well make the whole batch; freeze extra portions in small resealable plastic containers for later use.

Makes about 4 cups

24 dried red New Mexico chiles

4 cups beef stock, chicken stock, or water

2 tablespoons bacon grease, lard, or vegetable oil

2 cloves garlic, minced

2 tablespoons flour

1 teaspoon Mexican oregano

Salt

Honey (optional)

In a large cast-iron skillet over medium heat, toast the chiles on both sides (you'll have to do this in batches) until they soften slightly and become aromatic. When the chiles are cool enough to handle, remove the stems and seeds.

Transfer the chiles to a deep saucepan and pour the stock or water over them. Bring the mixture to a boil, then reduce the heat and simmer for about 10 minutes. Remove the pan from the heat and allow the chiles to rest, about 15 minutes.

Working in batches, puree the chiles with their soaking liquid.

In the cast-iron skillet, over medium heat, melt the bacon grease or lard, or heat the oil. Add the garlic and flour and cook, stirring, until the mixture becomes golden. Add the pureed chiles, and stir quickly while the sauce bubbles and spatters. Reduce the heat, add the oregano, and simmer for 5 minutes. Season to taste with salt. If the sauce is a little bitter, mellow it with about a teaspoon of honey, to taste.

New Mexico Green Chile Sauce

xxxxxx

Makes about 2½ cups

1 small white
onion, chopped

2 cloves garlic, minced

2 tablespoons lard or oil

1 tablespoon
all-purpose flour

2 cups homemade or low-
sodium chicken stock

1 cup chopped roasted New
Mexico chiles (stems and
seeds removed)

1 small tomato,
peeled and chopped

This is probably New Mexico's most famous recipe; it's what all visitors to the state remember. The sauce is best made with freshly roasted chiles (see Sources, page 86, and Roasting Chiles, page 33), but you can also use canned or frozen chiles. Pour leftover sauce over eggs, enchiladas, burritos, or tacos.

In a skillet over medium heat, sauté the onion and garlic in the lard or oil until soft.

Sprinkle the flour over the onion mixture and cook, stirring, until the flour becomes golden. Whisking constantly, pour in the chicken stock and continue whisking until it is completely incorporated.

Add the chiles and tomato, then reduce the heat and simmer about 15 minutes. Serve warm.

Guacamole Sauce

xxxxxx

Makes 2 cups

2 large, ripe avocados,
pitted, peeled, and
roughly chopped

¼ white onion, chopped

2 cloves garlic, chopped

1–2 jalapeños,
seeded and chopped

Juice of 1 lime

Water

Salt

Use leftover guacamole on fish tacos and inside bean burritos.

In a blender, puree the avocados, onion, garlic, jalapeños, and lime juice. Add just enough water to bring the sauce to a pourable consistency. Add salt to taste.

Peach Salsa

xxxxxx

Makes about 1½ cups

2 quarts water

2 ripe, but firm, peaches or nectarines

¹/₂ cup diced red onion

1 teaspoon crushed chile pequin or chile Caribe

1 tablespoon lime juice (or more), to taste

Salt

This light and refreshing salsa is one of my favorite accompaniments to tamales filled with red chile and pork. It offsets the denseness of the tamales, and the flavors blend together perfectly. Eat any leftovers with tortilla chips.

Bring the water to a boil in a medium saucepan. Slice a shallow 1½-inch-long "x" in the base of each peach or nectarine. Gently add the peaches or nectarines to the pot of boiling water and cook about 30 seconds, just long enough to loosen the skins. Use a slotted spoon to transfer the peaches or nectarines to a plate. When they are cool enough to handle, slip the skins off, starting from the "x" in the bottom of each, and dice the fruit into ½-inch cubes.

In a bowl, toss the peaches or nectarines with the onion, chile, and lime juice. Add salt to taste, and serve at room temperature.

Smoky Chipotle Salsa Roja

xxxxxx

If your tamales turn out drier than you had expected, you can throw this salsa together in a flash and tell your guests a tamale isn't a tamale unless it's positively slathered *with the stuff. It's a lie, but what's worse?*

Heat the lard or oil in a heavy-bottomed saucepan over medium heat and add the onion, garlic, tomatoes, and chipotles. Fry the mixture, stirring constantly, for 5–10 minutes, until the sauce has thickened. Season to taste with salt and serve warm.

Makes about 2½ cups

1 tablespoon lard or vegetable oil

1/2 cup diced white onion

1 clove garlic, minced

1 can (15 ounces) crushed tomatoes

2 chipotles in adobo, minced

Salt

Salsa Verde

xxxxxx

This bright, tangy salsa is used not only as a sauce for cooked tamales; it is also combined with chicken or pork to make a flavorful tamale filling.

Put the tomatillos and enough water to cover them in a medium saucepan; bring to a boil, reduce heat, and simmer 15 minutes.

Drain the tomatillos, and, in a food processor or blender, puree them with the garlic, onion, jalapeños, and cilantro. Add a little water if needed to make a smooth puree.

Add salt and sugar to taste. Serve immediately.

Makes about 2 cups

1/2 pound tomatillos, husked and washed

Water

2 cloves garlic

1/4 cup chopped white onion

2 jalapeño chiles, stemmed, seeded, and chopped

1 cup loosely packed cilantro leaves

Salt

Sugar

Black Mole

xxxxxx

Makes about 4 cups

4 dried chilhuacle negro chiles, stemmed and seeded, seeds reserved

3 dried pasillas chiles, stemmed and seeded, seeds reserved

8 dried ancho negro chiles, stemmed and seeded, seeds reserved

4 cups chicken or beef stock, or water

1/4 cup sesame seeds

1/2 cup peanuts

2-inch piece canela

6 whole cloves

6 allspice berries

6 cloves garlic

1 small white onion, peeled and sliced into rings

2 medium tomatoes, roughly chopped

2 tablespoons dried Mexican oregano

1/2 cup dried plums or raisins

1 slice challa, brioche, or other kind of egg bread

2 tablespoons lard or vegetable oil, divided

2–4 ounces bittersweet chocolate

Salt

Brown sugar

You may not be able to find all of these chiles, but as long as you find at least one kind of chile called negro *(black) or* mulato *(brownish-black), you'll be fine; aim for a total of 16 chiles. Sometimes I substitute a few guajillo or chipotle chiles as part of the mix; dried chipotles would give the sauce a smoky flavor. Yes, the sauce is complicated—but believe me, it's worth the effort.*

Preheat a gas or charcoal grill to high heat. In a cast-iron skillet set on the grate, cook the reserved chile seeds until blackened. (You can do this inside, but the fumes are pretty powerful!) Scrape the seeds into a small bowl and bring everything back inside.

In a saucepan over medium-high heat, bring the stock or water to a boil.

In a cast-iron skillet over medium heat, toast all of the chiles on both sides until they soften slightly and become aromatic. Transfer the chiles to a medium-sized, heat-safe bowl, and pour in enough of the hot stock or water to cover. Keep the chiles submerged with a small plate or saucer.

Add the sesame seeds, peanuts, canela, cloves, and allspice berries to the skillet. Toast, stirring, until the nuts are golden and the spices become aromatic. Transfer the mixture to your blender.

In the same skillet, cook the garlic and onion until the garlic turns slightly golden and the onion picks up some gold and black patches. Add the tomatoes, Mexican oregano, and dried plums or raisins, and cook until the tomatoes release their juices and thicken. Add the mixture to the blender.

Add the bread, soaked chiles, and about ¼ cup of the blackened chile seeds to the blender and puree, adding enough stock or water to make a thick, smooth sauce.

In a large, heavy-bottomed saucepan or Dutch oven over medium heat, melt the lard or oil. Add the pureed sauce and fry about 3 minutes, stirring constantly. Add the chocolate, stirring until melted; reduce heat and simmer, about 20 minutes. Season to taste with salt and brown sugar.

Mole Amarillo

xxxxx

Makes about 4 cups

4 cups chicken stock or water

6 dried amarillo or guajillo chiles

4 whole cloves

1/2 teaspoon cumin seeds

1 medium white onion, diced

4 cloves garlic

1/2 pound tomatillos, husked, washed, and quartered

1/2 pound yellow or orange tomatoes

2 tablespoons lard or vegetable oil

1/4 cup masa harina

Water

Salt

Honey

This mild, sweet yellow mole sauce is used both as a tamale filling and as a sauce. If you can't find amarillo or guajillo chiles, you can substitute pasillas or New Mexico red chiles. The yellow tomatoes give this mole a beautiful color, so do try to find them; using yellow cherry or pear tomatoes is fine.

In a saucepan over high heat, bring the stock or water to a boil.

In a cast-iron skillet over medium heat, toast the chiles on both sides until they soften slightly and become aromatic. Transfer the chiles to a medium-sized, heat-safe bowl, and pour in enough of the hot stock or water to cover. Keep the chiles submerged with a small plate or saucer.

In the same skillet, toast the cloves and cumin seeds until aromatic. Transfer the spices to the blender.

Add the onion and garlic to the dry skillet and cook until the onions char a little and the garlic gathers some golden patches. Add the tomatillos and yellow or orange tomatoes, stir to combine, and cook over low heat, covered, until the tomatillos are cooked through, about 20 minutes.

Add the tomatillo mixture, the chiles, and their soaking liquid to the blender and puree completely. Press the mixture through a sieve set over a large bowl.

Add the lard or vegetable oil to the skillet, set over medium heat. Fry the tomatillo/chile mixture for 2 minutes, stirring constantly, then add the remaining stock and simmer 5 minutes. In a small bowl, mix the masa harina with just enough water to form a smooth paste. Whisk it into the mixture and simmer 20 minutes longer, whisking often.

Season to taste with salt and about a teaspoon of honey, to taste (if the tomatillos were very tart).

Mexican Chocolate Ganache

xxxxxx

This addictively delicious sauce tastes much more complicated than it is. Pour warm leftover sauce over ice cream; or let it harden, then roll it into balls, and dust with cocoa powder for quick Mexican Chocolate Truffles. Or do what I do and eat the entire bowl with a spoon!

Put the chocolate in a medium bowl.

In a small saucepan over medium heat, bring the heavy cream just to a boil, then immediately remove it from the heat and pour it over the chopped chocolate. Let this sit for 5 minutes, then stir it with a whisk until all the lumps are melted and the sauce is smooth. Stir in the Kahlúa (if using), and pour the sauce over sweet tamales or serve them in a pool of it.

Makes about 1 cup

2 tablets (3 ounces each) Mexican drinking chocolate (Abuelita or Ibarra), chopped

1/2 cup heavy cream

1 tablespoon Kahlúa (optional)

Dulce de Leche

xxxxxx

Makes about 1½ cups

1 can (14 ounces) sweetened condensed milk

Here is an unbelievably easy way to make dulce de leche (meaning "milk candy"), a rich, intensely sweet sauce that can be drizzled over tamales, ice cream, poached pears, grilled bananas, or almost anything you can think of. The sauce will need to simmer for about 3 hours, but make sure you check it every half hour or so and add boiling water, if necessary. The can must be kept fully submerged or it might explode—and that would really ruin your dessert.

Put a rack or collapsible vegetable steamer in the bottom of a large saucepan. Rip the label from the can of milk and put the can on the rack. (If you want to make a large quantity of dulce de leche, you can boil several cans at once in your tamalera.) Pour enough water into the pot to cover the can by at least 2 inches.

Bring the water to a boil, reduce heat, and simmer for at least 2 hours for a thinner sauce, or up to 4 hours for a thicker sauce. Turn the can every 30 minutes or so and add water, as needed, to keep the can submerged.

Let the can cool completely before opening. The sauce will keep for a week, refrigerated in a resealable plastic container.

Atole and Hot Chocolate
xxxxxx

Atole

xxxxxx

Atole *is a warm, thick drink made from the same ground corn used to make tamales. In Mexico, where it is made in countless flavors with fresh fruits, it is a popular breakfast item in markets and cafes. In the Southwest, atole is less common, although some people still make it at home, and many will recall atole from childhood. Some restaurants now serve atole, and you may see it served very thick, as a porridge; it has the same mild flavor as grits, but a much smoother texture. Many people enjoy atole very plain; I like it with a little cinnamon and maple syrup. This basic recipe is ready for your innovations. Try adding in a little homemade strawberry preserves, frozen blackberries, pineapple chunks, or guava paste.*

Serves 4–6

1/2 cup masa harina

Pinch of salt

1/2 cup cool water

5 cups water

3-inch piece canela, plus 4–6 longer pieces for garnish

1 vanilla bean, split lengthwise

Honey and/or brown sugar

Put the masa harina and salt in a small bowl and add the ½ cup of cool water, stirring to smooth out any lumps.

Pour the 5 cups water into a saucepan set over low heat and whisk in the masa paste. Add the canela and vanilla bean and cook, stirring, until the mixture thickens slightly, about 10 minutes.

Allow the atole to cool slightly, then remove the vanilla bean and canela. Pour the mixture into mugs, garnish with canela sticks, and serve with honey and brown sugar on the side, allowing your guests to sweeten it themselves.

Blue Corn Atole with Piñon Nuts

xxxxxx

Serves 4–6

½ cup blue corn masa harina (or blue corn atole)

1 pinch salt

3½ cups water, divided

2 cups whole milk

3-inch piece canela

1 vanilla bean, split lengthwise

¼ cup piñon nuts, toasted (see page 15)

Honey and/or brown sugar

In New Mexico, where blue corn is a treasured native crop, it is easy to find blue corn tortillas, blue cornmeal, and, yes, blue corn atole. Often, blue corn masa harina (flour) is labeled "atole," so look for it under both names. I like to make this atole with milk. A warning from experience: if you put boiling-hot atole in your fancy stainless-steel travel mug—thinking you'll drink it on the way to work—it will burn a hole right through your tongue. To be safe, let the atole cool to drinking temperature, then *put it in the travel mug.*

Put the masa harina and salt in a small bowl and add ½ cup of water, stirring to smooth out any lumps.

Pour the remaining 3 cups of water and the milk into a saucepan set over low heat and whisk in the masa paste. Add the canela and vanilla bean and cook, stirring, until the mixture thickens slightly, about 10 minutes.

Allow the atole to cool slightly, then remove the vanilla bean and canela. Pour the mixture into mugs, garnish with piñon nuts, and serve with honey and brown sugar on the side, allowing your guests to sweeten it themselves.

Homemade Mexican Hot Chocolate

xxxxxx

Both hot chocolate and atole *are traditional accompaniments to tamales. Mexican hot chocolate is far, far superior to the American version. First, they make it from real chocolate. (How hard is that?) Then, they spice it up with canela, vanilla, and sometimes a kick of chile. Yes, you can buy Mexican drinking chocolate tablets (Ibarra or Abuelita brands), but if you can't find them—or you want something a little more interesting—try this method for making your own. If you can't find ancho chile powder, try regular old red chile powder; just don't use a powder that contains anything except ground chile peppers. And if you happen to have a little Cointreau lying around the house…*

Serves 4

5 cups whole milk

1 tablespoon (or more) ancho chile powder

1 vanilla bean, split lengthwise

3-inch piece canela

8 ounces unsweetened or bittersweet chocolate, chopped

Honey and/or brown sugar

In a medium saucepan over medium heat, combine the milk, chile powder, vanilla bean, and canela. Cook just until it comes to a boil, then reduce the heat to low.

Add the chocolate and whisk until it dissolves.

Remove the vanilla bean and canela, then pour the chocolate into mugs. Serve the chocolate with honey and brown sugar on the side, allowing your guests to sweeten it themselves.

Champurrado

xxxxxx

This is the sweet and delicious love child of hot chocolate and atole. You could call it chocolate atole or thickened hot chocolate, but most people just call it champurrado. *You can also make this with soy milk, skim milk, or just plain water. If you're really adventurous, add a little red chile powder to the masa harina!*

Put the masa harina and salt in a small bowl and add the ½ cup of water, stirring to smooth out any lumps.

In a saucepan over low heat, combine the milk and remaining 1½ cups of water. Whisk the masa paste into the saucepan and continue stirring until the mixture thickens slightly, about 10 minutes.

Add the chocolate and continue whisking until the mixture becomes thick, smooth, and velvety.

Allow the champurrado to cool slightly, then pour it into mugs and garnish with the canela sticks.

Serves 4

½ cup masa harina

1 pinch salt

½ cup cool water

2 cups whole milk

1½ cups water

3-ounce tablet Mexican drinking chocolate (Ibarra or Abuelita), chopped

4 long pieces canela (for garnish)

SOURCES

www.cookingpost.com
This Native American–run site is an excellent source for cornmeal, hominy, and other Native American ingredients.

www.buenofoods.com
Bueno's Autumn Roast is the best commercial frozen green chile you can buy.

www.melissaguerra.com
A great selection of dried chiles, herbs, spices, and more.

www.mexgrocer.com
Look here for enameled tamaleras, tamale-making kits, books, and ingredients.

www.nativeseeds.org
A nonprofit organization preserving regional indigenous and heirloom crops; carries a wide array of chile powders, dried chiles, and corn products.

www.loschileros.com
A New Mexico–based company that sells dried chiles, blue corn, and other items.

www.gourmetsleuth.com
Masa harina (including blue corn masa), corn husks, tamaleras, chestnut puree, and huitlacoche.

www.herbsofmexico.com
A huge selection of herbs and teas.

www.penzeys.com
Spices, spices, and more spices. Plus some chiles.

www.adrianascaravan.com
An excellent source for hard-to-find chiles and other ingredients.

www.markys.com
Miami-based purveyor of gourmet ingredients, including chestnut puree.

INDEX